THOUGHTS
IN
VERSE

Other Books by Dale Christensen

Patriot's Path (2014)
– a plan for our future

Dark Horse Candidate (2014)
– autobiography

Guide to Greatness (2014)
– inspiration to bring out the greatness in everyone

A Disciple's Journey (2014)
– spiritual perspective and religious background

10 Secrets To Speaking English (2001)
– method of helping people to speak a new language

Out of Print:

The Shopping Center Acquisition Handbook (1984)
– complete process and documentation

Turning the Hearts Vol. I-IV (*1982*)
– family history from earliest ancestors to marriage

History of the Church in Peru (1991)
– selective personal and general highlights

Entrepreneur Guide: The Ultimate Business & Learning Experience (2001)
– textbook for MBA course

Teaching Improvement Program
– USTC MBA Program & Business School (2001)
– training for MBA professors

THOUGHTS
IN
VERSE

5TH EDITION

BY

Dale Christensen

Thoughts in Verse
5th Edition

Published by:
Dale Christensen
Books@Dale2016.com

Book design and layout copyright © 2014 by Dale Christensen

ISBN
Hardback: 978-1-942345-16-9 - $29.95
Softback: 978-1-942345-17-6 - $29.95
eBook: 978-1-942345-18-3 - $10.95
Audio: 978-1-942345-19-0 - $10.95

Printed in the United States of America
Year of first printing: 2014

Dedication

To Edger A. Guest,
the Norman Rockwell of poetry,
and all the others who enlighten the soul
through sharing their thoughts in verse and prose.

And to my faithful wife, Mary-Jo:

A Goddess of beauty,
A modern Helen of Troy,
A lover of poetry,
A source of great joy.

Her life and character is every bit a poetic masterpiece.

TABLE OF CONTENTS

X. TRIBUTE

XI. MISCELLANEOUS

About the Author

The author, Dale Christensen, is the son of Irven Christensen who was a learned man who appreciated good thinking wherever and whenever it could be found.

His mother, Esther, always loved to read, collect, and memorize poetry.

This volume is an effort on the author's part to express thoughts in verse; hopefully good thoughts and good verse.

Preface

"Words do not convey meaning.
They call them forth."
- President David O. McKay

"Poetry restores to words
their power to evoke presence."
- Marcel

I.
ALLEGORY

TRUTH IS LIKE AN APPLE

An apple is an apple,
    No matter what the way
You choose to eat or cut it,
    Or the price you have to pay.

It may be green and bitter,
    Or very sweet and red.
It may be large and shiny
    Or withered, small and dead.

You can carve that apple nicely
    Or just leave it there to rot.
You can bake it in the oven,
    Or stew it in a pot.

You can share it with a neighbor
    And make a real friend.
It's what you do with it
    That matters in the end.

Now truth is like that apple,
    It's very plain to see,
Whether in your hand at present
    Or in a distant tree.

So hold to the fruit of wisdom,
    And seek the simple truth;
For wherever it is found,
    The truth is still the truth.

ORANGES

An orange is an orange is an orange,
    First small and hard and green.
When ripe and sweet, to be recognized
    Needs only to be seen.

Sweet fruit with juicy pulp
    Awaits expectant lips.
Satisfaction guaranteed,
    With eager gulps and sips.

But when it's served or eaten
    Uncut, un-sliced un-squeezed.
Taste buds tart with acid,
    Lips burned that go unpleased.

For all who love an orange
    It's good to give and take,
But do it right, do it best,
    For everybody's sake.

Both the giver for the giving,
    The taker here to stay,
Increasing in the bargain
    Or going on their way.

An orange is an orange is an orange
    'Tis true this fact remains.
But, how it's served and eaten
    Determines loss or gains.

PLANNING AHEAD

I love to feel the crinkle
    Of leaves upon the ground,
And smell the freshness of the air
    With beauty all around.

I love to watch the squirrels
    Running to and fro,
Storing up their winter's food
    While others southward go.

They're filling up the chimney tops
    Of trees above the town,
With treasures for the winter days
    When snow is coming down.

They chatter to their neighbors
    And stare as I walk by.
Then, with twinkling eyes they scamper
    So fast they seem to fly.

He's such a hardy fellow,
    An industrious little beast.
That we should follow his example,
    T'would be to say the least.

So for life's bitter winters
    And for future rainy days,
Let's plan ahead like they do.
    In the end, it always pays!

THE UGLY CATERPILLAR

Life's days oft make us, one and all,
    Bend in anguish to a crawl;
Like the caterpillar, sure to be,
    A butterfly so swift and free.

When in our heart. there's pain and hurt,
    All we see is grass and dirt.
How we long to upward fly,
    Enjoying high views from the sky.

But, tightly a cocoon we 'round us fold,
    Against harsh winds so bitter cold.
While the desire to live we slowly kill,
    In this jacket so quiet and still.

Here we could stay and wither up,
    Not drinking from life's bitter cup;
Always unhappy and in a fuss,
    Refusing what life has to offer us.

There's nature's pain in pangs of birth,
    Troubling all who share this earth.
Cause us to stir and squirm about,
    Struggling hard and worming out.

The moment we think the battle's lost,
    Desire's value surmounts all cost.
For in a moment when our tears are dry,
    We'll find ourselves a butterfly.

THE WHITE ROSE

The rose, with heaven's fragrance
That blossoms pure and white,
Reflects celestial grandeur
Of love, and truth, and light.

It symbolizes virtue,
Faith, hope and charity.
It represents Christ's perfect life,
And God's love for you and me.

Its beauty is a tribute
To God's creative hand.
It flatters all of nature,
And beautifies the land.

It's heavenly spirit matter,
The stuff from which it came.
Progress is its trademark,
And patience is its name.

This sacred, holy flower
Has meaning, and it should.
It represents the richness
Of all that's pure and good.

ROSE AND AMBER

I want a window to look out of,
   One of rose and amber pane,
Illuminating memories
   Of yesterdays not in vain.

Promising full tomorrows
   With rainbow hopes of things to be.
Do you have this wonder window?
   Would you share this glass with me?

II.
ATTITUDE

ALWAYS SAY I CAN

Life brings a daily challenge
    Each one of us must meet.
How we meet that challenge
    Brings success or mere defeat.

It doesn't really matter
    If the task is great or small.
Your attitude determines
    If you rise or if you fall.

So think of possibilities
    And always say "I can."
And life's challenges will find
    A happy succeeding man.

COMMON THOUGHT

It's a common thing to think a thought
    Of things we are and things we're not.
In deep despair one starts to sink
    If we entertain such thoughts to think.
But if we change the way we think
    We'll always rise and never sink.
We'll create our world and love a lot,
    For such is born in common thought.

FREEDOM

As I look out through prison's gate,
    I wonder now if it's too late.

For me to escape and then repent;
    Or is my life all spoiled and spent?

Can I break through these windows barred,
    To help the ones whose lives I've marred?

If I give back the things I took,
    Will the marks erase from my life's book?

Or once I've played the devil's game,
    Will I never be the same?

Then I heard a voice so true and strong,
    Saying to me, "My son you're wrong.

"Before you're free of vice and sin,
    You must rebuild your life within.

"To your surprise you soon will find,
    That your only prison is your mind.

"For once you're master of your thought,
    You'll have the freedom that you sought."

NEVER GIVE UP

My heart is heavy, my spirits are damp.
　I am discouraged and all forlorn.
I've hurt my friends or family.
　0, why was I even born?
I've stubbed my toe and fallen down.
　I just can't seem to get a goin'
I see the errors and mistakes I've made,
　And my sins are all a showin'.
"The only way," I've heard some say,
　"To get up and keep a pluggin',
"Is to rally and fight with all your might,
　And stand up and keep a sluggin'.
"The worst sin of all is to stumble and fall,
　And give up without even tryin'.
"To say there's no use or you don't really care
　Is the same as outright lyin',"
That's enough for me, for I clearly see,
　That this isn't the end of the fight.
It's only one struggle in a bigger battle,
　That brings victory into sight.

THE NEXT TIME

The next time I run, I'll win the race.
The next time I love, I'll not disgrace.

The next time I ache, I'll not cry out.
The next time I'm blue, I will not pout.

The next time I'm tested, I will not cheat.
The next time I repent, Twill be complete.

Oh yes, the next time I start anew,
I will be sure to follow through.

But, what of now before it's too late;
Shall I do it now or Procrastinate?

PAYING THE PRICE

You want the best in life you say,
But are you willing the price to pay?

It's freedom you seek so you can live,
But what is it that you're willing to give?

Do you compromise and just say, "OK,"
Or demand much more for a better day?

If you settle for less, I'm willing to bet,
You will deserve just what you get!

It's a law of life: "One seldom gets more
Than what he's willing to work and pay for."

For one thing is certain and this I know,
"You'll only reap just what you sow."

RESOLVE

Today started out so perfectly
    And ended up in chaos.
I think the Devil got a win
    And I chalked up a loss.
But it's a new day tomorrow,
    So we're gettin' up and tryin'.
We're not givin' in to him,
    Even if we think we're dyin'.
Thank you God for givin' us a chance
    To set our lives in order.
We need these moments to ourselves
    To think and reconnoiter.
It's truth we seek
    And right we must be doing.
So now we pray at the end of day
    So we can be renewing
Our covenants to thee this day
    To travel the narrow path so straight,
And hold to the iron rod so firm
    Before it grows too late.

SPEAK ENGLISH EVERY DAY

As little children, we learn to speak
With our tiny tongues, so very weak.

Then we learn to read and write
And study these with all our might.

Then one day the teacher says,
"A new language we'll learn these days."

So English words we study now
With grammar rules to teach us how.

To master all we need to know
To study abroad 'Cause we want to go.

The years go by one by one.
Sometimes 8 or 10, but they are no fun.

Because our tongues are still so weak;
Only to read and write, but not learn to speak.

We're all so sad and it's not 'til when
We are given Secrets from 1 to 10.

With these we can say what we want to say.
Our English improves by speaking every day.

There's only one way to train a tongue that's weak,
And that's everyday: just speak, speak, speak!

TAKE A BREAK

When the day seems short and hurried
    And you feel all undone,
Just stop and give yourself a rest
    And have a little fun.

If in your daily labors
    Your back begins to ache,
Just stand up and look around
    And give yourself a break.

Weak or strong it matters not,
    You need a frequent breather.
Because, if you work yourself to death
    You'll end up being neither.

That doesn't mean a man
    Should loaf or up and quit.
I'm merely trying to recommend,
    You stretch and breath a bit.

So when the day gets sort of hectic
    And you feel all undone,
Just stop and give yourself a rest
    And have a little fun.

Tell yourself a joke or two
    And laugh a little while.
Then return to meet the challenge
    And go the extra mile.

19

TAKE A LOOK

As I step aside to look at me,
  I'm oft' ashamed at what I see.

It seems to me when life is good,
  It's easy to do the things I should.

When in my heart, no trouble is found,
  When my mind is clear and my body's sound,

And my feet are warm and my stomach's full,
  It's not hard at all, for my load to pull.

It's a merry tune I whistle loud,
  Just strutting around and being proud.

But, when trouble comes and things go wrong,
  Do I forsake that tune for a sadder song?

When good fortune turns and my body needs,
  Do I lose my faith and neglect good deeds?

When my love is rejected by a broken heart,
  Do I hate instead or fall apart?

When life gives me a test, am I already beat?
  Do I work and study or do I cheat?

Well I've seen enough, so I will return
  To meet life's challenges to live and learn.

For one thing is certain and this I know,
  We always reap just what we sow.

TRIALS

Repent and live, return the borrow;
   Give up evil, guilt and sorrow.
      It's here today and gone tomorrow.

The truth is fact. You cannot hide -
   Joy and pain can both abide
      In one's heart, side by side.

To talk the talk will show the way,
   But it's not enough just words to say.
      One must walk the walk throughout the day.

Have faith to see beyond the night.
   Press forward with your inward fight
      Personal quest brings dawn's pure light.

If one's natural self is to be tame;
   Your will and choice, desire and aim,
      Belief and action must be the same.

Do your best and heaven send
   Your prayer of thanks and blessings lend,
      But most of all, endure trials to the end.

Reach out to others in their sorrow
   What strength you have, let them borrow.
      Your burdens will be gone tomorrow.

TWO SIDES TO LIFE

There are two sides to life. Which shall we choose?
　　The one that will heal, or the one that will bruise?

We're always confronted with evil and good;
　　Forever deciding if we shouldn't or should.

If it's right to be loyal or leave and forsake,
　　If it's better to give and not always take.

Do we have faith in God, or is it gold that we seek?
　　Are we puffed up in pride, or humble and meek?

Do we resolve to do right and make up our mind
　　To repent of our sins and leave them behind?

Are we a good neighbor going one mile more,
　　Or is helping them out too big of a chore.

Well, there's victory in life and there's also defeat.
　　We chose if we're honest or if we will cheat.

God in his wisdom will bless and rejoice
　　When each of his children makes the right choice.

So remember both sides, for between them you choose;
　　The one where you'll win or the one where you'll lose.

III.
HOLIDAYS

CHRISTMAS DAY

Once again on Christmas Day,
The bells peal out above.
The Lord renews for all of us
His precious gift of love.

Oh, may that blessing light the day
And all our hours fill
With every Christmas happiness
Of love, peace and goodwill.

MERRY CHRISTMAS

I wish to you, with lots of cheer,
A Merry Christmas and a Happy New Year.

My tongue's not sharp and my wit's not keen,
But I hope you get just what I mean.

'Cause to my recollect, we could all do worse,
In readin' trash that's not pure verse.

So in our lives, from time to time,
May we take to heart these words that rhyme;

Lovin' our neighbors and all that's good,
Doin' the things we know we should.

CHRISTMAS EVERY DAY

If Christmas ended sharply
    When clocks chimed midnight twelves;
Me thinks I'd rather go and be
    One of Santa's little elves.

Cheering the kiddies one and all,
    Aiding the old and gray;
To work and help to bring about
    A Christmas every day.

The age of twelve or ninety-two,
    It matters not at all.
If in your heart you're Santa's elf,
    You can have a year long ball.

Oh, what a long year it would be
    If all we did was wait;
For one short day of love and cheer,
    One eve to stay up late.

Only one happy season where
    The spirit of giving was high;
And bustling crowds in the square,
    Find the perfect gift to buy.

Christmas comes but once a year,
    This small fact I know.
But in our hearts it can remain,
    Through sunshine, rain and snow.

GIFTS

Of all the spirit children,
　　He was number one.
To Our Heavenly Father,
　　Christ was His grandest son.

He was the valiant spirit
　　Who formed the earth from clay,
And led us all to victory
　　Over angels gone astray.

He guided Father Adam,
　　Noah, Jacob, Moses and then;
Taught them all to worship,
　　And gave commandments ten.

We too were in His presence,
　　Long before our birth.
We rejoiced and sang Him praises
　　On the eve He came to earth.

The wise men and the shepherds
　　All came to celebrate,
The birth of our dear Savior,
　　In evening hours late.

Gifts of splendid treasures
　　Were brought to him that night,
But none compared to the gift of love
　　In the hands that held him tight.

Now, we can share some nice things,
 Just like the stories told,
But gifts of love and happiness
 Will outweigh the myrrh and gold.

May we give the gifts like he gave
 That last when we grow old.
For the kinds of gifts like he gave
 Are the kind that are not sold.

HOME FOR CHRISTMAS

The Christmas bells are ringing from Tokyo to Rome,
    And songs are being sung by those returning home.

Thoughts of all the kiddies and those now old and gray,
    Make our journey shorter and lengthens out our stay.

Friends we've long been missing, we'll have a chance to see;
    To share adventures of our lives and laugh and shout with glee.

It's not only just the visit that turns us homeward bound,
    But that special Christmas spirit that makes our hearts resound.

For going home for Christmas gives all of us a lift.
    For going home for Christmas is indeed a special gift.

THANKS BEGINS WITH GIVING

Thanks begins with giving, each and every day;
The best of ourselves to others, in work or fun and play.

'Tis true that word and deed treasure joys beyond compare,
But to be part of real Thanksgiving, the feeling must be there.

For the words that are long remembered, those so true and kind;
Are the thoughts that grew to action, and died not in the mind.

And a deed, in helping others, though quiet and small might seem
Is the thanks we can be giving if we'll act and not just dream.

Many a blessing is ours to count; bounties great and small.
Thanks to our Father who gave us life, and a Brother who saved us all;

For the freedom and the heritage we have and loved ones near and far;
For food we eat and clothes we wear, for the house and for the car.

God gives so much to you and me. Large is our debt to pay.
Just thanking won't pay the bill. We must act on what we say.

With sincere thought and action, happy we may live.
Of ourselves, we give to others, but to God 'tis thanks we give.

TO MY WIFE

I write this poem to my faithful wife
  Who inspires my heart and enriches my life.

You feed my soul and nourish my mind.
  You're a treasure indeed, greater than any find.

It is you I honor and this tribute I give
  That will stand as a symbol for as long as we live.

It's a simple message packed with emotion
  Of undying love and faithful devotion.

Stay true to your call your role divine,
  And if I am worthy you'll always be mine.

VALENTINE

No arrow can carry the wishes I share;
    Nor pigeon relay the message I bear.
A car is not able, a plane is too slow,
    And a train cannot hold all my precious cargo.
Telegrams can't kiss through miles of line,
    And a letter can't say, "Be My Valentine."
But, I can do all things that others can't do.
    I can take true love and give it to you.

MISS VALENTINE PRINCESS

Miss Valentine Princess, a right charming young lass.
    You rate a front seat in most anyone's class.

Like a goddess of beauty, a modern Helen of Troy,
    A seedling of greatness, a source of great joy.

You have all my prayers and my best wishes too,
    As I, with great pleasure, share my love with you.

31

Dale Christensen

WILL YOU BE MINE?

I want to write a poem of love
  With inspiration from above.

My pen won't write the things I feel
  When my head spins 'round like a wheel.

I just can't make my feelings flow
  To words that set your heart aglow.

I'd like to say, "You're fair to see,"
  But then you might just scoff at me.

I'd like to say, "You're quite a prize,"
  But then you'd blush and close your eyes.

So, I'll just wait my Valentine,
  And only say, "Will you be mine?"

IV.
HUMOR

THE BACHELOR'S BUG

There's a rampant epidemic
    Among the male sex.
Its effect is very simple,
    Yet it's miserably complex.

It seems to be disastrous,
    More potent than any drug.
I've often had the sickness,
    It's called, "The Bachelor's Bug".

The symptoms are only felt by those
    Wearing trousers and a shirt.
I've diagnosed their cause as one
    That's dressed in blouse and skirt.

It's fatal yet it isn't,
    Malignant yet benign.
No matter how bad your case is,
    It can't be worse than mine.

It seems like it's contagious,
    Then sometimes you'd wonder how
But, the only ones who spread it
    Are the ones who have it now.

Some catch it from a heartache,
    Others catch it from their pride;
Some, from their freckles or baldness,
    Or being too short or wide.

But, no matter how you catch it,
    The effect is still the same;
Your manhood flies out the window,
    And you're scared of every dame.

Now, there's a cure for every sickness,
    And for this, there is one too.
So, to rid yourself of bachelors bug
    This is what you do.

Keep warm and friendly always.
    Search for the one you deserve
Recognize worth and virtues,
    Exercise faith and serve.

Drink lots from the ocean of wisdom,
    And eat plenty of humble pie.
Learn that the cure for true love
    Is something you cannot buy.

See that your strength is sufficient
    To give what she will need.
Your ability to do this will determine
    Whether or not you succeed.

Once you're cured of Bachelor's Bug,
    There's others you'll contract.
But, of them all, this is the worst.
    'Tis pure and simple fact.

EATING HABITS

People's eating habits
   Are the ways they eat their food.
Some people laugh and giggle,
   Others sit and brood.

Some folks pick and nibble,
   Others stir and mash.
Some just sip and sigh
   While others slurp and splash.

Lots of people in a rush,
   Eat in quite a fury.
They always spill and waste more time,
   As they try to hurry.

To some, eating is a sport
   Of intense competition.
They practice in-between their meals,
   By constant repetition.

A very few are quite polite,
   Trying for improvements.
To them, it's all a symphony,
   With notes, and chords and movements.

"What we eat is what we are."
   'Tis a must we do it.
But as important to us all,
   Is how we eat and chew it!

JUST CHECKIN' ON YA

The nice old lady, wrinkled and poor,
  Bought her goods at the grocery store.

Her cart was full of fine cut meats,
  Vegetables and fruits and delicious treats.

The tall handsome clerk bent low to shout,
  "Thank you Madam, may I help you out?"

With a smile and wave, as she turned to leave,
  She said, "Sonny," as she tugged on his sleeve.

"It's you nice folks I need to thank,
  Since they won't cash my checks anymore at the bank!"

LIFE'$ BU$INE$$ $CHOOL

The professor began by saying,
    "Welcome to school ladies and gentlemen.
"You all are here to learn the trick
    Of making dollars grow from one to ten.

"With just a few $imple lessons,
    You'll learn this $killful art.
"The first lesson is your tuition.
    This is where you get your start.

"We'll take your precious money,
    Then teach you $ecret things
"That will turn your heart and $oul
    To all that money brings.

"You will learn the consumption function,
    And how computers make workloads light.
You'll learn how diplomacy and posturing
    Will help in the boardroom fight.

"Two courses on Money and $pending,
    Then to work on a Penny Purge.
"And you're ready for the Inflation Relation,
    And the $urge in the Urge to Merge.

"After your course on Tax Evasion
    And Finding Loop-Holes in The Law,
"You can learn to lie and swindle,
    And to rob your ma and pa.

"Now that will be your course of study,
    For this tidy little sum.
"Here's your receipt, now don't you cheat
    As you go through our fine curriculum."

DAD'S EMPTY BOXES

My dad collects these boxes
    From all the local stores.
With some, we hardly make it through
    Our over crowded doors.

He stacks them to the ceiling
    And all along the walls.
He fills them full of everything
    From trash to raggy dolls.

The pictures and the bills we paid
    Date back to '98.
All the things he's loved so much,
    I've now begun to hate.

It's not that I don't care to save
    Or find these relics out,
It's all the empty space we store
    That turns me inside out.

I've thought and wondered how
    To solve this task of ours.
So here's the plan I have,
    From long and thoughtful hours.

It seems so very simple,
    And I think it's very fair.
Just store you gold and jewels,
    And not your share of air!

V.
MANKIND

AMISH FRIENDS

I stepped back in time for a couple of days
    To visit with friends of the Amish ways.

What "peaceful, even feelings" came as I went hence.
    Their faith, love and strength I saw, and common sense.

Their pace and simple style of travel, work and dress
    Allows them time to really live and other lives to bless.

By sweat of brow and toil their gentle seeds are laid.
    Their food is grown and served, their clothes and tools made.

Was it back in time I went to live and feel and see?
    Or was it a real glimpse of how life ought to be?

As I watch the days busy by, as sunlight always ends,
    I often yearn to be more like my special Amish friends.

ANDY DRAKE

If we were the ones to pay the cost,
Of life's great battles won or lost,

'Twould be great help and very nice,
If someone else could pay the price

For our mistakes and all the rest,
In helping turn things for the best.

But, we must recall the Golden Rule,
Which reminds us that our role is dual.

Giving we must for another's sake,
To save the soul of an Andy Drake.

For of ourselves we soon shall see,
We are all that boy, or soon may be.

From pleasant dreams we might awake,
To bear the cross of an Andy Drake.

So let's each be a gracious host,
And befriend the ones who need us most;

And avoid the cost of the terrible mistake,
Of martyring the soul of an Andy Drake.

IT'S ALL IN WHO YOU KNOW

I've often heard the old ones
    Make this very claim,
As they gave the credit
    Or pass around the blame,

"For rising to the top,
    Or staying down below,
When it comes right down to it,
    It's all in who you know."

As I've pondered this thought,
    Morning, noon and night;
Even though it's simple,
    I think they may be right.

For when you're doing business
    And you want to make a deal,
It always helps to know the man
    Who owns the corporate seal.

Or if you're dating Nelly
    And wondering what she said,
It never hurts to know
    Her little brother Ned.

"It's all in who you know?"
    That could be very true.
Especially when it comes right down
    To knowing the real you.

And when you're sick and dying
   To be soon beneath the sod,
It never hurts to know the Man
   That everyone calls God.

You too will be admitting
   That everywhere you go,
What it boils down to,
   "It's all in who you know."

BODY AND SOUL

The body only grows to fit and clothe the real us.
The spirit is the stronger one who makes the real fuss.

The body tries to master all the days it lives,
The lessons that are given, those the Master gives.

The spirit, it is willing, but, oh, the flesh is weak.
We need the gospel "School Marm," to get the strength we seek.

Humor brings us gladness and courage makes us bold,
But its amount does not depend on if we're young or old.

Our mouth reminds us of our thirst and our hunger we can feed,
But only God can give us love, the kind we really need.

It's the stuff that makes us happy all our long life through,
And comforts us in sadness that hurts both me and you.

So to my body and spirit, I give this humble plea.
"Learn to get along you two, and then you'll be just me."

GETTING AHEAD

You asked a question once of me as you criticized my day,
But merely told me off and quickly went away.

You didn't seem to listen to a word that I had said,
I answered to your question of how to get ahead.

The answer isn't simple as my answer might imply,
But it's basic to the question of how to live and why.

Love God, ourselves, and others is the key, the Savior said,
In opening up eternal doors to help us get ahead.

Vanity, pride, and power with contention and conceit,
Are the real harmful things that bring our self-defeat.

Getting ahead in life, my friend, doesn't come from pomp and show;
But how and why we live our lives and the way we choose to go.

KEEP THE GATE OPEN

If you keep your heart open to truth and goodly deeds,
   You'll never be found wanting for filling others' needs.

If you keep your arms open to friends and loved ones dear,
   You'll always be found happy if they're either far or near.

If you keep the door open for one who broke your heart,
   You'll be getting ready for a brand new start.

If you keep the gate open for the lamb who's gone astray,
   He'll surely hear your gentle call and someday find his way.

LIFE AND THE PURSUIT OF HAPPINESS

Life and the pursuit of happiness
　　Are the goals our Father gave.
It's faithful living and pursuing
　　That mark the righteous and the brave.

Yes, faith builds up our courage,
　　And repentance makes us strong;
While the Holy Spirit guides us
　　As our journey goes along.

Eternal laws can govern
　　Our lives with peace and joy,
And snuff out all the venom
　　Of seething cankers that annoy.

Sacred groves we can discover
　　If our lives in balance rest,
And appreciate the good in life,
　　Both the poorest and the best.

Life and the pursuit of happiness
　　Are the goals we can attain.
And faithful living and pursuing
　　Earn rewards that will remain.

STATE OF AFFAIRS

It's true the wide world over,
    We're in a sorry state.
It causes us to wonder
    If it isn't now too late;

To change the course of history
    From the evils we endure,
To a world full of people
    Whose lives are rich and pure.

Can we turn the tide of vice,
    Theft, murder, rape and crime,
Unhappiness and divorce,
    And gambling in our time?

Halt economic peril
    With recessions many woes,
And stop inflation's spiral
    And get off welfare doles?

Or solve the fuel crisis
    Both domestic and abroad;
Stop the rise in taxes
    And trends that lead to fraud?

Cease religious confrontations
    Or racial prejudice,
And political corruption
    That lead the world amiss.

Will we cease to war and struggle
   With the peoples of the earth,
Or save the lives of infants
   And give them rights to birth?

Can we stop the violence
   That's shown on our TV,
Curb abuse of drugs and drink
   And all pornography?

Can we cease to pollute and waste
   For ecology's demands;
Will we feed the starving peoples
   At home and in distant lands?

While communism thrives,
   In this the eleventh hour,
On suppression's aftermath
   And threat of nuclear power;

On faulty education
   And broken family ties;
On lack of faith in God
   And truth twisted into lies.

We keep enacting gun laws
   And paying the CIA.
It seems for sure, that it will
   Catch up with us some day.

(continued)

Big government and big business,
   Apathy, sin and hate,
Seem to paint the picture
   Of what will be our fate.

Can we turn the world around?
   Can we change our destiny?
Yes, by following the Master,
   We can once again be free.

THROUGHOUT ALL ETERNITY

Father, Mother, I love you so.
My only wish is for us to go

To Heavenly Father's sacred home.
For there, we'll never be alone.

Deep in my heart, I feel the pain.
Of never seeing you again.

But, if we're sealed to one another,
We can live with Christ, our brother.

To grow in love and perfect be
United throughout all eternity.

Dale Christensen

TIDES IN THE AFFAIRS OF MEN

The waves roll in with thundering tide,
   And then retreat as winds subside.

Such are the affairs and lives of men.
   Good fortune comes in and goes out again.

We're often stranded on lonely sands,
   But we're never lost from God's own hands.

The spirit is gone, the way seems dark;
   We know not the course on which to embark.

This is the plan of our mortal life,
   We're exploring worlds of struggle and strife

It's His own way of building souls
   Of men searching for eternal goals.

TRUTH

I know it sounds so simple
And may seem so very bold,

But one never finds unless one seeks.
That's what we have been told.

YOUNG AT HEART

As hand in hand we go along,
    Enjoying life together,

May we always sing a song,
    And stay young at heart forever.

WORDS OF WISDOM

A word to the young, a word to the wise,
    Don't fall prey to cunning lies.

You can't be strong and walk real tall,
    By trying to smoke or drink alcohol.

You can't get rich and pay your bills,
    By smoking joints or popping pills.

True joy and peace will pass you by,
    If you're shooting up and getting high.

Your troubles won't pass, your friends won't stay,
    And your body and mind will waste away.

So, if you want strength and want to be wise,
    Don't fall prey to cunning lies.

These Words of Wisdom are brief but true,
    Their test of worth is now up to you.

WORK

God said to man that work was good,
    And by your sweat you'll do it.
So bend your back and push along
    And never wait, just do it.

Adam taught his many kids
    To work six days in seven.
Pay their tithes and tend to church,
    And pray they'd get to heaven.

He showed them how to sacrifice
    The firstlings of their flock.
By carving it a special way,
    And roasting it on a rock.

God was pleased with Adam's work
    So he kept him for quite a while;
To raise his kids as he knew right,
    To do their share and go the extra mile.

Work will cure most any ill,
    From heartache to depression.
But, how to do it doesn't come
    In just one single lesson.

Now why can't we, a few years hence,
    Learn and do this same thing over.
Instead, it's leisure that we seek,
    But very soon we find we're planted under clover.

WORTH OF A SOUL

How many men have walked a mile,
    One hundred or a thousand if need be,
To find their fortune, their glory or pride;
    To conquer the mountain or sea?

How many have given life or limb,
    Or a better part of their soul,
For a diamond, a treasure or even a purse,
    Or a trophy for winning a goal?

If so many have run this kind of race
    And paid the prices required,
Why haven't more helped others in need
    Instead of quitting when tired.

The worth of a soul is greater than all
    The riches we all can combine.
This is the measure our Savior taught
    As he left the ninety and nine.

VI.
NATURE

THE COMMON COLD

The common cold I hate so much
    Is such an awful pest.
It keeps me from my daily chores
    And robs me of my rest.

The sniffles and the runny nose
    Always tickles and annoys.
But, the coughs that come with sneezes
    Make a joke of grace and poise.

The fever makes my head split up
    A thousand different ways.
I'm always dizzy standing up
    Or lying in a daze.

My bones and joints and muscles,
    All throb with aches and pains.
But, even with the doctor's help,
    The common cold remains.

The only thing that seems to help,
    Is to know that others share
The aches and pains and fevers
    And the feelings of despair.

So, when you're spry and healthy,
    It's wise I have been told,
To guard against the clutches
    Of that darn old common cold!

CONDOR PASSES

In ancient Andes Mountains
  The Condor lives alone.

It eats the flesh of animals
  Leaving alone the bone.

High it flies and circles
  To find its food and prey.

It doesn't hurt the living -
  It only eats dead things each day.

It sounds a little morbid,
  But it's really quite serene

It eats up Nature's garbage
  And keeps the country clean.

Dale Christensen

EDEN'S LUSH GARDEN GREEN

The lush green meadow pastures
   With streamlets crystal clear,
Both full of life and light
   Not knowing hate or fear.

Then quietly creeps in an evil
   And changes white to gray.
Confused, then tempted in the choice
   Means being sent away.

Just a little, simple thing
   Can cause a giant change
In our heart or in our actions,
   And our future rearrange.

It's always just a moment
   Or just across the way
That the pasture seems the greener
   To tired eyes that stray.

It's often in our anger,
   Neglect or slothful pride,
That we lose our lofty vision
   Or run away and hide

From the oasis in the desert
   That gives us life and light;
To lesser styles of living
   That rob us of our might.

Yes, mighty volcanic eruptions
    Can spread both stone and ash
Across our fertile prairies,
    And hopes they quickly dash.

So hold to the rod of iron,
    And walk the path you're on.
It's easier not to leave it
    If you'll stay where you belong.

THOROUGHBRED

Born to be a champion, born to keep the pace,
    Born to be a thoroughbred, born to win the race.

Racing is its purpose, winning is the goal.
    Of each mighty charger, beginning as a foal.

MOUNTAINS

No one knows the story
    Of how mountains came to be,
Or how they grew in splendor
    From deep beneath the sea.

We know so very little,
    A notion at its best,
That God created matter
    And time has done the rest.

Not knowing all the details
    That mother nature hides,
We can still enjoy the colors
    And the rhythm of the tides.

We can bask in golden sunlight
    Beneath the sky so blue,
And see the royal jewels
    In the early morning dew.

We can dance along the prairies,
    And swim the everglades.
But, in climbing up the mountains,
    Our courage quickly fades.

There is something very special
    About their rugged majesty,
That makes us wonder how they came
    From deep beneath the sea.

Towering in the lofty clouds,
   Rising high above the land;
They tell the story of the world
   Because they saw it all firsthand.

WHAT CAN I GIVE?

What can I give to ease the pain,
When you are discouraged from being lame?

Can I bring a flower or share a gift,
To give your spirits that needed lift?

Can I give you a hug or even a pill?
If that won't do it, what else will?

I guess I can always try to share
With you, the thought that others care.

Oh, yes, that's the thing I'd like to tell,
In wishing that you could soon get well.

PASSING OF A DAY

Each morning of the earth's life, stirring from where she's lain;
The movement is slow but steady to the showers in the rain.

With sunshine, warmth and vigor, all budding out with zest,
She throws away the old clothes to wear her summer's best.

And painting on her make-up of emerald green it seems,
She adorns herself with jewels of sparkling crystal streams.

As the day progresses, growing and having fun,
Miss Earth is very fruitful as she's basking in the sun.

But fun and play is not enough. There's a lot of work to do
During the fleeting hours beneath summer skies so blue.

When late afternoon approaches and cold becomes the breeze,
Lady Earth puts on her golden coat heavy laden to the knees.

Soon the day is over and all the work is done,
And lying down to rest awhile brings sleep in the setting sun.

When Mother Nature tucks her in, she finds to her surprise;
Earth didn't take her clothing off before she closed her eyes.

So quickly taking off her clothes and leafing them aside;
She turns the heat down low, then spreads them far and wide.

Then snowflakes fall from heaven to clothe her body brown
In a glistening robe of splendor, the most beautiful evening gown.

And white sheets and blankets to cover and to keep
Her snug and cozy all night long 'till she wakes up from her sleep.

VII.
DATING

KNOWING YOU WERE NEAR

On that first day, I thanked the Lord
    For life and liberty;
For all His love and many gifts
    That He had given me.

I had good health and happiness, and things
    That I could share.
I had the gospel, my family's love,
    And many friends who'd care.

I could not ask for another thing
    But a tender, loving wife.
And that's the way I felt that day
    You walked into my life.

My heart sang out when my eyes beheld
    The girl I'd longed to see.
I saw you pause, then slowly walk,
    Then soon you talked to me.

My heart began to whisper when
    Our eyes would often stray.
As you listened while I tutored you
    In chemistry that day . . .

Were you my princess, my dream girl,
    My Florence Nightingale?
That cheerful, dancing fairy I've been chasing
    Over hill and dale.

I wondered then if you could be
    My valiant Joan of Arc.
Were you the light I'd searched for,
    Shining in the dark?

These questions would be answered
    Within the coming year.
Its true, I thanked the Lord for seeing you
    And knowing you were near.

LOVE

Love is tender, love is divine;
I love you, please be mine.

LOVE'S STORY

There's a story told I'd like to tell,
    Heard in the ring of a chiming bell.

The same is whispered when soft winds blow,
    And carefree waves dance to and fro.

The theme is one of love and care,
    One easy to have but hard to share.

This story is told by most everything,
    From earth to heaven where angels sing.

Its brilliance compares to the noonday sun,
    When its little light, sparks a special one.

It's a novel or poem, both verse and prose,
    That thrills one over from head to toes.

It's a song that grows more loud and true
    As one speaks the words "I love you."

Now, the story's told, and I hope you've heard,
    Though others think it a bit absurd,

To listen to stories and speak of love,
    From here on earth and sky above.

But, if you'll hear the words I say,
    I promise then to go away.

For I will know when I depart,
    Love's story will stay within your heart.

MEETING YOU

I've longed to climb the mountains high,
    And glide like birds up in the sky;

And run the forest wild and free,
    To taste and smell, to feel and see.

To swim the oceans like a fish,
    Was once to me my biggest wish.

I've even hoped to meet a king,
    And hear the choirs of angels sing,

To do great work for God above,
    And share the fruits of perfect love.

Yes, many things I've hoped to do,
    And one of them was meeting you.

Now that it's past, that great event,
    I'd like to share just what it meant,

By wishing the best in every way,
    To you my dear on this happy day.

MY THOUGHTS OF YOU

It has been a while since seeing you,
And I long to say your name.
Since I first shook your tender hand,
Life just hasn't been the same.

Remembering when I saw you first
On that great and glorious day;
I wondered if we'd ever speak
Or even find a way.

I wondered if I can last to see
Once again your tender smile,
To meet and talk then share some time
And linger for a while.

There's gentleness in your loving hands.
There is beauty in your face.
Your head is poised and gracious,
And you move with ease and grace.

I wanted to share these thoughts of mine,
But waited 'till I could clearly see
That you were indeed that "Special One"
Just waiting there for me.

POWERS OF LOVE

Only a flame just now, my little one,
    But, a fire it will be.
As the days go by with the passing sun,
    Love's glow you'll feel and see.

In the air all flames may bend
    And the flicker may be small,
But all flames have powers they lend,
    Three that move us all.

The first is that of light to see,
    The glow that lights our way.
The next we feel with joyful glee,
    It's the warmth for which we pray.

The third has magnitude of glory's height.
    It's the motivation of those who believe
Which guides the hearts of men aright
    To do all they can conceive.

My flame of love will ne'er go out
    As it flickers amid life's maze;
For you who kindle and bring about
    The roaring of a blaze.

THAT SPECIAL ONE

The flowers are many and sweet fruits divine,
    But I'll not taste of any 'till that special one's mine.

The shiniest of apples or the tastiest peach,
    Is high in the tree top far out of reach.

It's not shaken loose to fall from the tree,
    Because it's that special one just waiting for me;

To climb with precision and not just by chance ,
    To carefully pick it from that high lofty branch.

Its freshness I'll cherish and protect with my life.
    For such fruit is my goal in choosing a wife.

Such is the measure of each maiden's worth,
    Like the freshness of flowers that cover the earth.

Their fragrance is virtue to be guarded with care,
    Against those who'd pluck them in their sly, crafty snare.

Their beauty is priceless and if freely spent,
    'Twill leave their sweet petals all soiled and bent.

Such is the plight of those lining the road,
    Drooped under the weight of their dark, dusty load.

But, as I travel the world, it's you that I'll find,
    Not tarnished by others and then left behind,

But, far from the path when my searching is done,
   I will sit down beside you my dear special one;

And nurture the love that God meant to be ,
   For you see, special one you're that special to me.

MY 4 FAVORITE COLORS

Grasses are green and skies are blue;
   Sunshine warms me and so do you.

YOUR SMILE

As I woke up this early morn,
    I sighed a sigh and felt forlorn.

I rubbed my eyes then moved about,
    Sat up in bed and then got out.

I brushed my teeth then combed my hair,
    Brushing away each worldly care.

I dressed myself then shined my shoes.
    By then, I'd buffed away the blues.

Off to breakfast I went to eat.
    I'd begun the day, but still felt beat.

I tried to work for a little while,
    Thought of you and saw your smile.

The joy that's shared in your smiling way,
    Just lifted me up and made my day.

I can work and give and never tire
    With spirits lifted all the higher.

So when I wake and feel blue
    I'll close my eyes and think of you;

Hoping that if I dream awhile,
    You'll share with me your special smile.

VIII.
COURTSHIP

IF EVER TWO WERE ONE

If ever two were one,
  Then surely we can be.
So sacred is our love
  For all the world to see.

Remember us in friendship?
  Our hearts were wide awake.
We'd gladly give or sacrifice
  For one another's sake.

We found a special oneness
  In the Gospel plan,
And realized the meaning
  Of woman, and of man.

We learned how God our Father
  And Jesus Christ above,
Are perfectly united
  In power and in love.

With the Holy Spirit binding
  All our thoughts and deeds,
Inspiring us with wisdom
  And aiding in our needs.

Such oneness is a virtue,
  Of this I am so sure;
That our Heavenly Parents
  Share love so sweet and pure.

It's true that we are human
And need humility,
But if our souls are one,
Like them we too will be.

It seems so very often
That the veil seems to part,
And glimpses of eternity
Bring praises to my heart.

It causes little wonderment
When I hear your tender voice,
Through space and distance whispering,
"Commune and come rejoice."

Yes, in spirit we're communing
Through the whole entire day,
And in our dreams at nighttime
We laugh and joke and play.

We feel each other's feelings,
Tasting the bitter and the sweet.
We sense the other's nearness
And often times we meet.

Oh God, bless our growing oneness,
Like Thee we wish to be.
If ever two were one
Then surely we will be.

JUST ONE SWING

What I wouldn't do to have you here,
  My special love, my special Dear;

To gather you up, letting arms surround;
  To hold you close and swing you around.

Then sweep you off your feet I would,
  And hold you as close as I possibly could.

With your arms around my neck so tight,
  You'd laugh and scream with pure delight.

I'd spin and spin and 'round we'd go.
  I'd laugh and shout, "I love you so!"

There safely cradled in loving arms,
  You're free from fears and all that harms.

For moments, the world keeps rushing by,
  While we share a kiss and sigh and sigh.

After all this fun and spinning around
  I'd set you softly on the ground.

Then softly, gently, we'd hug and kiss;
  Sharing our love, our joy and bliss.

For this great treat so very nice,
  I'd work and toil and sacrifice.

I'd fight all beasts with my bare hands;
  I'd cross the desert's blistering sands.

I'd bear the winters snow and ice,
  For just one swing, 'Twould be so nice.

I'd search the jungles, walk on burning coals,
  Climb high mountains, swim rocky shoals.

No, there's nothing that I wouldn't do
  To share the thrill of swinging you.

You see, my dear, that's what you bring,
  To my heart that's yours, with just one swing.

GOD BE WITH YOU

God be with you, is my prayer,
As we journey along life's thoroughfare.

'Till we meet again, and our dreams come true,
I'll be thinking cherished thoughts of you.

There are many times we'll have to part,
And nurse the aches of our tender hearts.

But, this is the price we've chosen to pay,
For a chance to travel along life's way.

For as we journey, day by day,
Love's diamonds and rubies will come our way.

These jewels we seek are worth all cost.
For without these gems, our lives are lost.

So, God be with you, is my prayer,
As we journey along life's thoroughfare.

'Till we meet again, and our dreams come true,
I'll be thinking cherished thoughts of you.

MY DREAM AND YOURS

I have a dream I'd like to share,
  With you for whom I really care.

The result of it all we'll just wait and see,
  But now I'll try giving as you've given to me.

There are so many things we'll see come to pass;
  Things to share with you, my charming lass.

To let you feel what I feel you mean to me,
  And watch you grow to what you can and want to be.

I too have a lot to learn and do,
  A lot of growing to measure up to you.

You see there are giants in more ways than one.
  And you, my dear, many hearts have won.

Yes, in the sight of God and in the hearts of men,
  You're esteemed as one with the strength of ten.

You're endowed with great blessings from heaven.
  The world is a loaf and you are its leaven.

Oh, there is so much we cannot comprehend,
  So many riches above if we'll endure to the end.

But, it's a must you remember not to scare,
  If I'm a bit awkward in helping you there.

You see, I'm trying the key to your heart and its doors,
  In hopes that some day my dream will be yours.

MY DEAR MARY-JO

God bless you my love, my dear Mary-Jo.
  I want you to know that I love you so.

It's not just the words that are so dear,
  But their meaning to me that brings you near.

I kiss every kiss on the letters you seal,
  And cherish the way that you make me feel.

I'm asking you now if you'll always be mine,
  By asking you now to be my Valentine.

I'll give you Sweetheart all my special love.
  I'll give you the world and the skies above.

I'll give you forever as you can see,
  I'll give you my all, I'll give you me.

Together we'll search and find heaven's doors,
  If you will be mine and I will be yours.

MY SONG

I have a warm feeling way down inside.
    It gets so strong that I cannot hide
        It any longer.

Hear and feel as I've felt and sung,
    Those sweet chords in my heart have rung
        Deep down inside.

What I'm trying to say, is that it's true.
    My heart and soul is yearning for you.
        My love is yours.

Come to my side and stay with me,
    And the world together we will see,
        Your hand in mine.

MY PROPOSAL

These are my intentions, as I propose to Thee;
    To take Thy hand in marriage and live in unity.

Our eternal friendship has nurtured love divine.
    I've accepted Thy love, and Thou accepted mine.

Is there cause to tarry or justify delay?
    Can we afford to linger and both begin to stray?

If not, then here am I, bowed humbly on my knee.
    I love Thee, Oh my Darling, will you marry me?

YOU ARE

You are my love. You are my life.
    You are my friend. You are my wife.

You are my princess. You are my queen.
    You are beautiful. You are serene.

You are wonderful. You are my mate.
    You are the best. You are great.

You are patient. You are kind.
    You are poised. You are refined.

You are exciting. You are fun.
    You are a comfort. You are "My One."

You are my support. You are my desire.
    You are my flame. You are my fire.

You are His child. You are divine.
    You are my love. You are mine.

WHO'S THAT?

Gentle, sweet and softly spoken.
　　With will of steel and purpose oaken.

Painting memories of sculptured days;
　　Forging character and mending ways.

Inventing laughter building souls;
　　Climbing mountains and reaching goals.

Fighting battles, defending right;
　　Inspiring greatness, and sharing light

With neighbor, friend, sister, brother,
　　Child and stranger, father and mother.

Negotiating fairness and giving love.
　　Serving others and God above.

That's my girl I'll have you know.
　　If you haven't guessed--that's Mary-Jo!

IX.
MARRIAGE

MOLLY MORMON

(See Maude Muller by John Greenleaf Whittier)

Molly Mormon, on one fine Latter-day
  Flipped hamburgers in a most righteous way,
Beneath her hat glowed the wealth
  Of simple beauty and wisdom's health.
Singing; she thought, with merry glee
  That a temple bride one day she'd be.

But when she glanced up at the crowd
  She only saw bullies, brash and loud.
Her sweet song died, and a vague unrest
  And a nameless longing filled her breast;
A prayer, that she would one day find
  A faithful Elder who was true and kind.

A returned missionary just then passed,
  Paused and turned and quickly asked:
May I sit and rest here for a while
  And admire your eyes and lovely smile,
While you cook a burger for me to go?
  French fries and a drink, I'll let you know.

She went right to work and cooked it up,
  And poured water for him in a paper cup,
And blushed as she gave it, looking down
  At her uniform of yellow and brown.
"Thanks!" said the RM, "a better meal or sweeter drink
  "Could not be served by a fairer hand, I think."

He spoke of football, the Jazz, and the Bees,
Of hiking Mount Timp and climbing trees.
Then talked of tracting, and his companions old,
And asked her if she thought him too bold.
And listened while a pleased surprise
Looked from her long-lashed hazel eyes.

At last, like one who for delay
Seeks a vain excuse, he went away.
Molly Mormon looked and sighed. "Ah me!
"That I this young man's bride might be!
"He would take me to the temple pure
"And treat me like his queen for sure."

"Our family would pray both morn and night.
We'd never complain or argue or fight.
We'd go to church and serve each other;
Have a baby girl for every baby brother;
Pay our tithes, weekly date and do temple work
Home and visiting teaching we'd never shirk."

The young man looked back as he closed the door
And saw Molly Mormon across the floor.
"A form more fair, a face more sweet,
"Ne'er has it been my lot to meet;
"And her modest answer and graceful air
"Show her wise and good as she is fair."

"Would she were mine, and I today,
"Could propose to her and whisk her away.
"No more looking, no more blind dating

"No more emptiness and no more waiting.
"But true love and songs of birds
  "And health, and quiet and loving words."

But he thought of his sisters, proud and cold,
  And his parents divorce, over land and gold;
Almost closing his heart, the young man went on,
  Leaving Molly at McDonald's and he was gone.
He went back to work humming a love-tune;
  And Molly cooked burgers all afternoon.

She wondered if her old boyfriend could be
  The kind of a man she envisioned a husband to be.
But he wasn't active and he smoked and swore.
  He wasn't exciting, he was always a bore.
No, he wouldn't do now that she had found
  That there were better men coming around.

"Should I marry the girl who waited for me?"
  He thought, "My parents picked her my wife to be."
Then he thought of the poem of the Judge and maid,
  And declared right then not to let this spark fade.
He would not have such words of tongue and pen
  Be those saddest of words, "It might have been!"

So he dashed right back and got on his knee
  And asked Molly if his bride she would be.
It was short notice for they had just met,
  So a week from that day, the date was set.
They talked and they talked and dreams they shared.
  Their hearts told them both that they really cared.

They married and together they worked
  Not a duty or task or assignment was shirked.

She put him through college 'til graduation was near.
  Still the children they came about one every year.
The burdens were heavy and time was so short.
  He didn't take a break and she was a good sport.

They tried everything they could right from the start,
  But so many things were keeping them apart.
Slowly, oh slowly they grew old and gray.
  Love's light still flickered, but "Dimly," they'd say.
First it was poverty that challenged them most,
  But later on, prosperity tempted both to boast.

Gradually they seemed to be drifting away,
  And if it went unchecked, that way they might stay.
Why wasn't it working, had it all been a mistake?
  Before it's too late, another road should we take?
Within temple walls and with divine help unseen,
  The calm reassurance came to both so serene.

It's service, sacrifice, forgiveness and kind deeds
  That nurtures love's light and fulfills longing needs.
So brothers and sisters as you grow your love strong
  Never forget to help your companion along.
And when you think of your words of tongue and pen
  They won't be those saddest, "It might have been."

Instead you must be faithful and do it because
  You want the words, "It could have been and was!"
So priesthood brethren keep loves vision bright.
  By loving your wives always, day and night.
Ongoing service, repentance and love
  Will keep blessings coming from God up above.

MY BLESSINGS

As I count my blessings, you always come to mind,
   In returning from my journey, to you who stayed behind
To keep the home fires burning and care for those so dear.
   Your task is truly greater, I can see it very clear.

Your noble heart expanding with every deed you do.
   Your wisdom ever growing, always staying true.
You're always blessing lives in so many, many ways;
   Giving of your happiness on the cloudiest of days.

My work seems so unimportant, as I think of all the time
   I spend in chasing rainbows. It seems to be a crime.
Even though I travel to those places far away,
   And meet important people in every place I stay,

And learn the culture of that place or tantalize my mind,
   There's nothing like that thought of you
As you focus in my mind.
   I see the most enchanting face with twinkling eyes that shine.
Oh, I'm so very thankful that you are truly mine.

You're my life and everything. You're the one that I adore.
   I'll always call you blessed. I'll love you ever more.
So when I count my blessings, those extra special kind,
   You're the first and most important to come into my mind.

FIRST HARSH WORDS

"The first harsh words never need be spoken,"
Was the counsel to bride and groom.

They are Satan's tools that hurt and divide,
And bring to all sorrow and gloom.

So resolve this day to bridle your tongue,
And never drive loved ones apart.

Only speak softness in loving tones,
The feelings and thoughts of your heart.

OUR DAY OF DAYS

We rose to meet the sunrise,
    On this glorious day of days,
And knelt in sweet thanksgiving
    For Heavenly Father's sacred ways.

We entered His Holy Temple,
    And were sealed for all time.
To progress and grow together,
    And share our love sublime.

Again we kneel to ask the Lord
    For health and happiness.
It is our prayer as we now join,
    That our lives He'll richly bless.

WEDDING DAY

Marriage is God's gift they say.
    This I know is so,
For you who celebrate today
    Share love's radiant glow.

Through the long and lonesome hours
    And the dark and dreary nights,
May you always feel love's powers
    In knowing heavenly heights.

You must nurture love for each other
    And to the other be always true.
Your love has brought you together
    And your love will see you through.

The future can be the toughest trial
    With an empty life that's boring,
Or full of eternal joy sublime,
    One that's so rewarding.

The goals you set and roads you take
    Brings a paradise into view.
The joy you have in your married life
    All depends on you.

X.
TRIBUTE

DEAR HEIDI

I came to your home, one fall afternoon.
 Your parents took me in and gave me a room.

The sun has set at the end of your day.
 We think of you now, here where you lay.

We know your sweet spirit left your body for now.
 With grief and sadness our heads humbly bow.

We'll miss you dear Heidi until there and when
 We'll love you forever until we meet again.

Your body lies still in dear mother earth,
 While your spirit lives on just as before birth.

Brothers and sisters were we, before we came here,
 To family and friends who loved you so dear.

You got your own body so beautiful and bright.
 You were tested in choosing between wrong and right.

During your lifetime, you achieved so many things.
 Just the thought of it all to our hearts, joy it brings.

Your heart beat its last so your spirit could leave.
 Gently slipping away, leaving us here to grieve.

But, to you it was wonder! And joyous to meet
 All your dear loved ones gone before; now there to greet.

(continued)

Your reunion's so glorious, full of stories and love.
About those left behind and those up above.

We know you're so happy and will continue to grow,
But we'll miss you so much. We just want you to know.

That we'll love you dear Heidi, until there and then.
We'll love you forever, until we meet again.

WIVES

I write this poem to my faithful wife
Who inspires my heart and enriches my life.
You feed my soul and nourish my mind.
You're a treasure indeed my greatest find.

It is you I honor and this tribute I give
That will stand as a symbol for as long as I live.
Undying love and faithful devotion.
It's a simple message Packed with emotion.
Stay true to your call, Your role divine.
And if I am worthy You'll always be mine.

HERO FOREVER

Today is a day of tribute,
    And to you I wish to pay
The greatest tribute of them all
    On this very special day.

True happiness comes with giving.
    To you, each gift becomes a tool
In helping yourself and others
    Understand and live The Golden Rule.

You're charitable and wise, humble and sincere,
    Possessing knowledge for which men thirst,
A living legend of honest labor
    And considering others first.

I've watched your hands move mountains,
    And many forest and field you've tilled.
Countless minds you have enlightened
    And empty lives you've filled.

You've been my hero for a long time,
    Ever since I was just a kid.
Now I know I am so much happier
    For touching my life the way you did.

We've laughed and worked together
    And shared the fun in many a game.
I wish fond memories to always be yours,
    Though I seemed hard for you to tame.

Now I want noble thoughts to nurture,
    And many great deeds I wish to do;
Rejoicing in life eternal
    In bringing honor to Mother and you.

Father, you're a hero forever in my heart,
    As great as Socrates Moroni, or Lincoln.
Yes, you'll be a hero in my heart forever.
    I'm just proud to be called your son!

FAITHFUL SPOUSE

Some measure their worth in assets and liabilities
    Instead of friendship and love and eternal realities.

A man thinks he's strong if he can manage and direct,
    But if he really thinks this, he's foolish and wrong.

Great strength and true worth whether a man or a mouse
    Is determined largely by your sweet faithful spouse.

True blue forever she can make or break him
    She's his real strength the greatest asset of all
        With her, he's a very rich man.

COME AFTER US

Within the temple walls, painted with golden leaf;
  Overarching window, expressing their belief.

"The Lord has beheld our sacrifice, come after us" they wrote.
  A long time then forgotten; now, for all of us, to note.

Words that now are gone; we each can still be gleaning,
  Multiple lessons to learn with each and every meaning.

Perhaps they bid to follow their example true and pure
  Or come after them to Utah with lesser hardships to endure.

Perhaps their genealogy we must search and find.
  Or bring them back to Zion, all those who stayed behind.

Does it mean the last be first? Or shall the first be last?
  Is it rebuilding old Nauvoo as a tribute to the past?

Or to all the unborn spirits who soon will come to earth;
  Perhaps the real meaning is showing them their worth.

No matter what the meanings, all glorious and true;
  They left it there for us read, to ponder and renew.

MILLENIAL MOTHER

Fair maiden now with life so pure,
 Desire that's strong and faith so sure.

The noble call to you has come,
 To be a Mother in the Millennium.

Here and now, we prepare and wait;
 In these last days, as hours grow late.

For Christ the King to come and reign,
 And bring forth Zion to earth again.

You teach with care and share with love
 The noble spirits from heaven above.

Continue strong. Stand fast and sure.
 Have faith and work; all things endure.

Have joy and peace. Love one another.
 You're a Saint, a Millennial Mother

JUST THE SAME

Mother, you're a blessing
    From my Father above.
I only wish now
    I could express all my love.

For the woman of my life
    You will always remain.
Though I have a girl or a wife,
    I'll love you just the same.

I remember the sweet moments
    At your loving knee,
As you taught me the things
    That mean the most to me.

I remember lessons you taught
    Though scolding it was;
And the comfort you gave
    When my heart was abuzz.

Oh, the fun we'd have laughing,
    'Till we thought we would die,
Erased all the moments
    Of hurt when I'd cry.

Mother, you brought so much love
    Into our sweet little home.
I'll always feel near you
    Wherever I roam.

To you, Mother, I pay tribute
   With this small token of love.
It's my prayer I might share it
   With you here and above.

It's all of your faith
   That I now need,
To realize potentials
   Which are still in their seed.

All the things that are good
   I want to try,
So I can give you the best
   That money can buy.

So courage, my dear,
   Though Ester's your name,
Whatever I am,
   You're "Me Mum" just the same.

To express the feelings
   Of my heart all aflame,
Whatever Mother dear,
   I'll love you just the same.

OUR ELDER WHAT'S HIS NAME

The Mormon Elders come and go a dime a dozen here,
Then there's one who comes along you grow to love so dear.
At first he wins your heart away, with humble clothes he wears.
Then soon you grow to worship him, for he neither smokes nor swears.

He loves to talk of all the things in life so dear to you.
And, when he leaves you with a prayer you never feel blue.
He doesn't need his flannel board, the blackboard or the chalk.
For when he preaches from that Book you know it's Gospel talk.

He eats up all that's on his plate, and helps you on the farm;
And still it seems where're he's at, he has that certain charm.
He's just the thing you've hoped for in all the days gone by;
An example set for Junior, and for Sis, a sweetie pie.

Now everyone is growing so and always learning more,
Not to spoil the ones you love becomes your biggest chore.
Then it seems to happen no matter where they go,
When the dreaded transfer comes, it comes with quite a blow.

The sadness comes at parting time with long remembered tears.
And sacred are the letters, exchanged in future years.
And no matter how many Elders, to all of them I'll tell
The stories of the mighty one, the one you loved so well.

RENAISSANCE MAN

It's not very often there walks such a man
    That can truly be called a Renaissance Man.
Centuries have come and many have gone.
    Millions have lived and then passed on.
There have been but few, who've sojourned on earth,
    Who have risen to heights of noble birth.
But others have risen to heights unforeseen,
    With the unquenchable spirit of a renaissance dream.
The renaissance Man is of noble breed,
    Who builds men and earth by planting a seed.
He's a father, a husband, a truly good friend;
    To his own family he is a Godsend.
He's a healer, a builder, a leader of youth.
    He's a warrior, a martyr, a champion of truth.
He's a poet, a singer, a master with pen.
    He's a teacher, a hunter, a fisher of men.
He's a champion, a winner, the one in first place.
    He's a hero and leader to the whole human race.
He speaks words of wisdom and makes your heart burn,
    As he gives you his heart for nothing in 'turn.
He creates from chaos a true masterpiece;
    And from soiled torn rags, a fine golden fleece.
Each day lived to the fullest, from morn until night;
    He endures to the end, never quitting a fight.
Few men on earth can make the claim
    Of being that kind, or close to the same.
Only a few have known of this vital breath,
    As they've passed through life from birth to death.
Yes, it is seldom there walks such a man
    That can truly be called A Renaissance Man.

XI.
MISCELLANEOUS

COME TO MARYDALE

Come to Marydale now and celebrate
　　With us the great life, so why hesitate?

It's a special place, with moments in time
　　Where memories are made, making your rhythms rhyme.

It's an experience to keep, or with others to share.
　　It's a feeling that grows, once you've been there.

It's a place to relax, 'cause your hurry must wait
　　When burdens are left outside of our gate.

It's a place, and a time, wherefore, who and when
　　Good thoughts and feelings, to good deeds be then.

Breeze and warm sunshine will mix and will make
　　A lawn to a meadow, and a pond to a lake.

With delicious food, drink romance divine,
　　Dance, laugh and have fun, with non-alcoholic wine.

Enjoy peaceful slumber and such restful sleep,
　　Regaining your strength, and fond memories keep.

Yes, this is the place. By car, bike or bus,
　　Come to Marydale, "Come roost with us."

GOALS

I've set some very lofty goals
    To serve, to teach and save some souls.

The goals are clear the plans are sure,
    I must prepare myself by staying pure.

The scriptures offer the light I need
    To gather the flock or plant the seed.

By my example, I hope to set,
    I'll catch some men in the gospel net.

The priesthood power will bind them true
    And help them start their life anew.

My desire and efforts determine my success
    In reaching my goal or settling for less.

Now I just need to follow through,
    On the thing I know is true.

0

OSGOOD FILE: FRANKLIN QUEST CO.

Dr. Benjamin Franklin said, "Time is the stuff that life's made of."
Folks, you can't save it, you have to spend every minute you have
and they're not making any more of it!

Sir. Benjamin Franklin was really quite a man.
    Excelling in so many things by following his plan.

Franklin's quest you see was an odyssey in time.
    It holds the secrets of his life and a formula sublime.

Each and every one of us can learn these lessons too.
    Harmony brings balance productivity increases too.

"What is time?" you ask. "It's a simple thing," they say,
    But when you try to manage it, it quickly slips away.

St. Augustine tried his guess, but couldn't give a clue.
    Newton tried defining it, but then he lost it too.

Einstein came along and said, "Not so my honored gents.
    The universe is measured relative to events."

Mankind must work so hard in bringing home the bacon.
    "Controlling is the key," said Mr. Alan Lakin.

Increasing productivity and building self-esteem
    Is the thing to help us cross our personal "I" beam.

Adapt to what we cannot change and control the things we can.
    We're conditioned 'til our needs rise up and hit the fan.

Planning skills prepare the way to prioritize our tasks,
  "But how to implement the plan?" Is what everybody asks.

Just look at all the books with a well tuned scanner.
  Then get the best of what there is, a fine Franklin Day Planner.

We call it the pyramid a process everybody knows,
  And at it's base and upward are the values and the goals.

They help us focus on our tasks that mean the most to us.
  We give them A's, a B or C - 1, 2 3 saves us lots of fuss.

Check it off or delegate or forward it ahead.
  A dot shows it's in process. An X shows that it's dead.

One calendar keeps it all right before your face.
  It's magic how you have it all in just one single place.

When interruptions come and steal our time away,
  We know exactly where we are we never need to stray.

When we feel very tired and then procrastinate,
  We quickly solve the crises before it gets too late.

We learn to be proactive, and always be our best.
  We never loose a detail or clutter up our desk.

We eliminate the floaters and the time robbers too.
  Ben used this Franklin process. If I can, so can you.

(continued)

Commitment makes the difference. Good habits are a must.
  Customize your system and keep it in your trust.

Just call that (800) number or jump into your car.
  Come have a great time quest in a Franklin seminar.

It's easy to remember and not with others mix.
  Dial it now, don't you wait. It's (800) USA -1776.

SCHOOL

Little Johnny goes to school
    To learn his A, B, C's.
Sally's gonna make new friends.
    Both will fall and skin their knees.

There's lots to learn and understand
    And Mom and Dad are prayin'
That the teachers that will guide them
    In the school, will be stayin'.

It's hard enough to change each year
    And have to adjust all over.
From a different teacher in every class
    And bullies who push you over.

After grade school and junior high
    High school seems so hard.
No more fun and games to have
    Stress grows to improve the report card.

THE PROTECTOR

I was born and then I was two.
    I found a stick and I was a warrior true.

Then I was six and protected my maiden fair.
    I dreamed that I caught her when she fell through the air.

Then I was ten and challenged any outside my gang.
    I watched then played cowboys and war with a bang.

Then I was sixteen and fought at the goal line.
    To protect honor of city and school that was mine.

Then I was nineteen and went forth to proclaim
    And protect the truth and share with others the same.

Then I was twenty one and really fought in a war.
    To defeat aggression and preserve liberty near and afar.

Then I was twenty six and with marriage and bride
    I protected her alone and pushed all else aside.

Then I was thirty and my little ones came.
    I loved and protected them all the same.

Then I was forty and it was difficult to fight
    Protecting my family from evil, sin and moral blight.

Then I was fifty and the struggle didn't stop
    Still protecting from people clear to the top.

Then I was sixty and then seventy five.
  Protecting my health just to stay alive.

Then I was old and the time was now mine
  For protecting my soul for my reward divine.

NAMES

Names are but symbols for acquaintance.
  Honor given to us by our loving parents.

Too often felt by many as a hindering noose,
  Instead of a gift to be put to good use.

Name of self can only to us from another reflect.
  And from your own name, what can you detect?

MY TAMARA

A long time ago, together, we chose the Savior's Plan.
And fought the war in heaven against Satan and his clan.

You surely were my hero or a heroine to me,
For I promised to ever serve you and on earth your father to be.

Perhaps we were good friends before our mortal birth,
And promised to each other to remember our soul's worth.

Me thinks a guardian angel you've been the same to me.
And carefully watched over as I ventured forth to see.

Well, I came ahead of you to form a home of love;
To receive you and teach you from heavens above.

If you'd have been twins, you'd not been Jane or Laura.
She'd been Herta Day, and you'd been Dawn Tamar'a!

You've blossomed and you've grown to be a maiden fair.
You're spirit has prevailed despite my clumsy care.

Each day I thank the Lord for riches large and small.
And as I count my blessings, you're the greatest of them all.

Now is the time of giving. This Christmas season's bright.
I can't give gold or silver, but these gifts I give tonight.

My gift is simple counsel: be faithful, good and true.
My gift is simple love, that I freely give to you.

Please accept my humble offering, like the shepherds long ago,
And feel my love for you, while through your life you go.

TRAVELING

It's my own opinion that traveling's quite a sport.
   Whether you are flying out our sailing into port.
You can swim or ride a mule or even drive a bit.
   It doesn't matter if you hitch or if you're hoofin' it.
But, like I was saying, traveling's quite a game.
   Once you get the travel bug, you're never quite the same.
Here's tribute to the traveler, the gypsy passing through.
   You're the champ of travelers, I wish that I were you.

WHAT IS POETRY?

What is poetry? Please define it then.
   What makes a real poem, flow from your pen?
Is it word choice alone, or maybe the rhyme?
   Is it the music, which makes you feel fine?
So round and round, this discussion goes.
   Where will it end, none of us knows.

Some think that a poem, from words just then grows,
   But in the end, it's only just prose.
Words with their beauty, deep feeling and thought,
   Full of real meaning, but real poetry it's not.
For without real rhythm and without real rhyme,
   It'll just be nice prose, throughout all of time.

INDEX
Alphabetical Listing

www.ingramcontent.com/pod-product-compliance
Lightning Source LLC
Chambersburg PA
CBHW022026090426
42739CB00006BA/309